THE BRITISH MUSEUM
INDIAN
LOVE POETRY

THE BRITISH MUSEUM
INDIAN
LOVE POETRY

A. L. Dallapiccola

THE BRITISH MUSEUM PRESS

Frontispiece: Lady watching pigeons, from Guler, Panjab Hills, *c.* 1770. Gouache on paper. This painting conveys the brooding mood of a *virahini*, a woman separated from her lover. Filled with poignant memories of past intimacy, she gazes intently at the courting pigeons, with the stark background reflecting her loneliness.

© 2006 The Trustees of the British Museum

First published in 2006 by The British Museum Press

A division of The British Museum Company Ltd

38 Russell Square, London WC1B 3QQ

www.britishmuseum.co.uk

A. L. Dallapiccola has asserted her moral right to be identified
as the author of this work

A catalogue record for this book is available from the British Library

ISBN-13:   978-0-7141-2437-7

ISBN-10:   0-7141-2437-0

Photography by the British Museum Department of Photography and Imaging
Designed and typeset in Centaur by Peter Ward
Printed in China by C&C Offset Printing Co., Ltd

For Conrad Clark

and in memory of Elisabeth Lutyens
(1906–83)

Special thanks are expressed to
Richard Blurton and Sona Datta
for their patience, infectious humour
and support in the preparation
of this book

Portrait of Raja Balawant Singh listening to musicians, from Guler, Panjab Hills,
c. 1745–50. Gouache on paper. Inscription on right: portrait of Raja Balawant Singh;
on left: Ladbai is singing 'Oh my love, how you have tricked me . . . ' Raja Balawant
Singh (c. 1724–63) was a great art connoisseur and patron, and this portrait is by his
devoted friend, the painter Nainsukh. In contrast to the rather formal rendering of
Balawant Singh, who is leaning on his left hand and holding the pipe of the *huqqa* in
his right, the five performers are depicted as individuals, their distinct features and
gestures caught with immediacy and human warmth.

INTRODUCTION

'. . . Oh my love, how you have tricked me!'

These words are sung by Ladbai, the young woman depicted in the illustration opposite. She is dressed in brilliant red, with a *tanpura* in her lap, and her presence seems to fill the bare, uncoloured background, where there is no shape or colour to distract the eye or disrupt the restrained yet emotionally charged atmosphere that pervades the painting. Listening with rapt attention to every note of the music is Balawant Singh, a lone figure seated on a carpet who leans on his left hand while holding the *huqqa* pipe in the other. Nothing is known of either the poem or its author, but the despondent mood of the woman who utters this heart-rending line has been arrestingly visualized in the sparseness of this work. The themes of her song, of which only the one crucial line is quoted, are probably the pangs of love, deceit and hurt.

Love, both human and divine, is a major component of the poetic and literary output of the subcontinent's various languages. Of the nine main *rasas* or sentiments which form the basis of Indian aesthetics, *shringara*, erotic sentiment, is known as the king of sentiments (*rajarasa*). The most popular etymology of the word was suggested by King Bhoja (*c.* 1010–55), who described *shringara* as that through which a peak (*shringa*) is reached, probably referring to a climax of delight. There are two main kinds of *shringara*, of which the first is love in union (*sambhoga*), but the verse quoted above is a typical example of the more important kind, love in separation (*vipralambha*), which has been an endless source of inspiration both in secular and religious contexts.

In the wake of devotional movements which swept through northern India from about the fourteenth century, both Hindu and Muslim mystics interpreted *vipralambha* as an allegory of the human soul divided from God, personified by the *virahini*, the woman separated from her lover. They believed passionate devotion to God was the only means of salvation, and their verses often employed the language of love poetry. Composed in regional languages rather than Sanskrit (the language of the learned), their message of selfless surrender to a personal god (*bhakti*) carried an immediacy and vigour which had wide appeal.

These devotional movements were not merely a northern Indian phenomenon. What became known as the *bhakti* movement began in the fourth or fifth century in the region corresponding to the modern state of Tamil Nadu, where it developed and blossomed from the seventh to the ninth century. The language of these poet-saints was Tamil. Their impassioned compositions stress the importance of selfless love between man and God, which alone gives meaning and purpose to human life, offers freedom from sorrow, and eventually establishes the union of deity and devotee. The twelve *Alvars*, which can be translated as 'those who are immersed or drowning' (in God), were followers of Vishnu and included the poets Antal and Nammalvar, while the followers of Shiva, the sixty-three *Nayanmars* or 'chieftains', included Karaikkal Ammaiyar and Manikkavachakar.

From Tamil Nadu the *bhakti* movement spread to neighbouring southern Indian states and eventually to the north, both through migration of individuals and popular diffusion of the poems and their message. What is now the modern state of Maharashtra played a key role in this diffusion between the south and the north of the subcontinent. The cult of Vitthala (Vithoba in Marathi), an aspect of Vishnu, became prominent here in the thirteenth century and remains the most important local cult. Among the most famous followers of Vithoba was the seventeenth-century mystic Tukaram, whose poems are still sung by pilgrims on their way to the Vithoba shrine in Pandharpur.

One god in particular, Krishna, became the focus of north Indian devotion. His complex personality encompasses many aspects: the child doted upon by foster parents, his romantic entanglements with the shepherdesses (in particular with Radha, an affair vividly rendered in Jayadeva's *Gitagovinda* in the twelfth century), his role as friend and counsellor to the hero Arjuna in the great battle of the *Mahabharata*, and his position as a shrewd statesman and ruler. This range offered four different means of emotional approach. The devotee could imagine himself as Krishna's parent, friend, slave or lover. Predictably, this last aspect was the most popular: for instance, the Rajput princess Mira Bai saw herself as Krishna's bride.

Krishna's attraction permeated not only devotional but also courtly poetry. Considered the epitome of the refined courtier and consummate lover, Krishna was the paradigm of elegance and etiquette. One of the foremost of the courtly poets was Keshava Dasa of Orchha, whose *Rasikapriya*, a 'treatise' on love written in Hindi, is his most popular work. In it he seeks to explain love at first sight, how and where lovers meet and how passion affects men and women, and finally he speaks perceptively about lovers' sentiments including remembrance, pathos, fury and laughter.

The fact that the main actors of the *Rasikapriya* are Krishna and Radha rather than mere humans marks a departure from earlier literature on the subject, especially Bhanu Datta's *Rasamanjari*, a late fifteenth-century Sanskrit poem on which Keshava Dasa partly based his own work a century later. Radha and Krishna, the divine pair par excellence, became a model for human lovers in their courtship, misunderstandings, tiffs and eventual reconciliation, culminating in candidly described physical ecstasy. This gave both mystics and courtly poets ample scope for creating a vast body of poetry which, in turn, inspired painters to illustrate their verses.

The three or four main characters in both *Rasamanjari* and *Rasikapriya* are the hero (the *nayaka*), the heroine (*nayika*), her confidante (*sakhi*) and occasionally the hero's friend. The function of the *sakhi* is to carry messages and arrange meetings between the couple. She guides the often inexpert *nayika* through the intricacies of courtship and consoles her when she is lonely. Whenever the story takes a dramatic turn, it is the *sakhi* who tries to assuage the offended *nayika* and pleads the cause of the *nayaka*. She is the matchmaker, trying to bring about the union of the lovers in the face of the inevitable obstacles. As well as being a brilliant diplomat, the *sakhi* also comments in brief asides on the progress (or lack of it) of the love affair. The male friend of the hero, whose function is similar, appears relatively seldom. Holding centre stage is the *nayika*, with the *nayaka* in a supporting role.

The first known classification of the various types of *nayikas* is found in the *Natyashastra*, a Sanskrit treatise on the dramatic arts attributed to the sage Bharata and probably composed between AD 100 and 300. Bharata lists eight types of *nayikas*:

> . . . one dressed up for union, one distressed by separation, one having her husband in subjection, one separated [from her lover] by a quarrel, one enraged with her lover, one deceived by her lover, one whose husband is abroad and one who goes out to meet her lover . . .
>
> (XXIV, vv. 210–11)

All subsequent authors have adhered to this initial categorization without major alterations and it forms the backbone of Indian love poetry. However, additional classifications and sub-classifications, based on the age, status and degree of sexual experience of the *nayikas*, has further refined this framework, providing a highly structured analysis of human passion and revealing extraordinary insight into the psychology of lovers. Love poetry thrived and, inspired by the verses, artists painted remarkable sets to illustrate the *Rasamanjari*, the *Rasikapriya* and the *Nayaka-Nayika bheda*, a classification of heroes and heroines, which became the prized possessions of rulers and connoisseurs.

Keshava Dasa composed another extremely successful work on poetics, the *Kavipriya*, which contains a celebrated *barahmasa*, a set of twelve poems each describing a different month of the year with its own particular festivals and rituals. We hear only the voice of the woman who, while describing the charms of each month, pleads with her husband or lover to stay with her.

This literary genre has a long history. The oldest work, inspired by the six seasons of the Indian year, is a short work called the *Ritusamhara*, attributed to the great Sanskrit poet Kalidasa, who flourished in the fifth century AD. In it, the charms of the seasons and their pleasures are masterfully described, although the human voice is hardly heard. The earliest *barahmasa* quoted here is drawn from Mulla Daud's *Chandayana* (fourteenth century). The primary voice is that of the *virahini*, the woman separated from her husband or lover, who awaits his return. While wasting away in sorrow, she poignantly describes her lonely life, contrasting it with that of her happily settled friends. The *barahmasa* from Jayasi's *Padumavati* (1521) is similar. Both poets were Sufis, and for them the *virahini* is almost certainly a symbol of the human soul, pining for union with God. There is no clear resolution in a *barahmasa*: we never know if the *virahini* will be reunited with her lover or whether the elegant beau of Keshava Dasa's *barahmasa*, depicted as Krishna, will leave his wife to go on a journey.

The *ragamala* ('garland of *ragas*'), a unique form of painting, developed from a combination of sources including the codification of musical modes and the poetry attached to each mode, describing the appropriate time for each melody to be performed — which season, day or night — and, most importantly, the mood to be conveyed. The most common format of a *ragamala* album comprises six male *ragas* and their six or seven wives, the *raginis*, making a total of thirty-six or forty-two poems and paintings. There are, of course, regional variations: for instance, *ragamalas* from the Panjab Hills have sixty-four leaves illustrating *ragas*, *raginis* and their offspring, the *ragaputras*.

The earliest rudimentary forms of *ragamalas* are found in fifteenth-century western Indian manuscripts. This genre developed and flourished over the following centuries, mainly in northern India from the Panjab Hill states to the Deccan. Recently, however, *ragamalas* from further south such as Wanparthi (Andhra Pradesh) and Mysore have been discovered.

In the fifteenth-century manuscripts, the *ragas* and their *raginis* were visualized as deities, and the accompanying text is a mere *dhyana*, a brief meditational stanza describing the appearance of the deity. However, from the sixteenth century the texts evolved into poems of varied lengths describing love situations, and painters happily followed this new trend. The main sources of inspiration for *ragamala* texts are the various *nayikas*, the *barahmasa* and the Krishna myth. The poems describe the excited anticipation of a love tryst (Vilavali *ragini*), love in union (Dipaka *raga*), the heroine remembering past love encounters (Asavari *ragini*) or love in separation (Vangala *ragini*). In these paintings the *virahini* is shown as an emaciated ascetic either performing penance, reciting mantras or simply sitting in the wilderness with a tiger as her sole companion. The *barahmasa* and Krishna themes coalesce in Hindola *raga* and Vasanta *ragini*, which celebrate the onset of the vernal seasons: Krishna sits on a swing with his beloved or plays *holi*, squirting colours on a bevy of young girls, or dances in their midst carrying a tender sapling in his hand, a symbol of the renewal of life. In the monsoon *raga* Megha Mallar, Krishna appears in a forest glade under a dramatic stormy sky, dancing ecstatically in the pelting rain. With him are two girls, one beating a drum and the other keeping the rhythm with a pair of cymbals.

The legacy of the past is still very much alive: the poetry of the great Sufi masters still stirs a strong emotional response among visitors to Sufi shrines all over India. In Tamil Nadu, the hymns of Alvar and Nayanmars are still regularly performed, cherished and memorized. Parts of Antal's *Nachchiyar Tirumoli* are sung at Tamil weddings, and well-known soloists interpret the hymns of Manikkavachakar at great temple festivals. The hymns of Mira Bai, the *abhangas* of Tukaram and the poems of Sur Das are also very much part of the living tradition and frequently arise in everyday conversation.

The India Book House in Mumbai has published an extremely successful series of comic books about Indian mythological and religious personalities, among which feature most if not all of the poet-saints quoted here. Contemporary painters such as Laxman Pai have drawn inspiration from, among others, Bihari Lal's poetry. Classic films explore the lives of the great devotees such as Tukaram (1936) and Mira Bai (1945). More recently, the life of this remarkable woman saint has inspired Kiran Nagarkar's historical novel *Cuckold* (1997), in which he vividly recreates the mood of the times while describing Mira Bai's life through the eyes of her husband.

The month of Chaitra (March/April)

The charming creepers are in bloom and once more the trees are young, covered in blossoms. Flowers fill streams and pools; elegantly dressed women, burning with passion, abandon themselves in the enjoyment of love. The parrot, the maina and the cuckoo warble songs of love. In such a charming season, no-one should embrace the thorns of separation, abandoning the flower of union. Why think of going away?

Keshava Dasa

Page from a dispersed *barahmasa* series from Bundi, late 17th century. Gouache on paper. On the left sit a couple under an awning. He holds a flower in his hand and she gives him a *pan*, while an attendant stands in the background with a fan. The ground floor of the mansion is occupied by a large bed, furnished with bolsters and pillows and surrounded by various flasks, spittoons, *pan* boxes, flowers and perfume containers. On the right, in a more modest establishment, a woman also offers *pan* to her lover. In the right foreground is a lake filled with lotus flowers which teems with birds and fish. Between the buildings is a riot of flowers, foliage and creepers in bloom, and peacocks, peahens and other birds are flying off into the sky.

The month of Vaishakha (April/May)

The earth and sky are filled with fragrance: a gentle, sweet-smelling breeze blows softly. Beauty is everywhere and perfume pervades the air, inebriating the bee and filling with longing the heart of the lover far from home. I beseech you, who have made me so happy, not to leave me in the month of Vaishakha. The arrows of the love-god Kama are difficult to bear during separation.

Keshava Dasa

Page from a dispersed *barahmasa* series from Bundi, late 17th century. Gouache on paper. A couple sit on a terrace outside a room with a large bed and two bolsters. They are engaged in an animated conversation while two attendants, one with a peacock's feather swish and the other with a fan, stand in the background. In the foreground two men, one armed with bow and arrow and the other with a sword and shield, walk along the shore of a lake. A third man, having removed his turban, sits in the shade of a tree, fanning himself with a leaf. Behind the brick wall are orchards and lush gardens. Hidden in the fronds of a tree, a diminutive Kamadeva, the god of love, aims his flower arrows at the couple on the terrace. At the foot of a banyan tree a group of ladies worship the Shiva *linga*. Two peasants draw water from the lake with the help of a pair of bullocks, while a gentlemen's party glides past on a pleasure boat.

His pointed arrows are the young flowers of the mango; the string of his bow is a line of bees. Oh my beloved, the warrior of spring comes to conquer pleasure-loving hearts.

KALIDASA

Detail from page of a dispersed *barahmasa* series from Bundi, late 17th century. Gouache on paper. The god Kama emerges as a diminutive figure from the crown of a tree. His flowery bow and lotus-tipped arrow are clearly visible as he aims at the couple on the terrace. The love-god is said to be armed with five arrows (for the five senses), and his helper and ally is the spring season, Vasanta.

The month of Jyeshtha (May/June)

Air, water, ether, earth and fire — all these five elements become one: a blazing fire. The wayfarers are exhausted and the elephants become tame, seeing the dried-up pool. The cobra slithers up the elephant's trunk and the tiger lies in its shade. All creatures on earth and in the water are restless and weak. This is why the wise enjoin lovers not to leave home in this season.

Keshava Dasa

Page from a dispersed *barahmasa* series from Bundi, late 17th century. Gouache on paper. In the heat of the summer a couple seek respite from the blazing sun inside a makeshift pavilion of aromatic grasses and matting. Two attendants wave their fans energetically in a vain attempt to create a breeze, while a third carries a tray of flower garlands and, in her hand, a bottle containing a cooling perfume. Around the mansion are water channels, a cascade and numerous spraying fountains. In the foreground birds bathe in a lotus pond, a tiger lies exhausted in the shadow of an elephant, and a cobra slithers among the grasses. A group of weary travellers rest beside the wall of a lush garden. Inside a Persian wheel raises water from a well to feed a fountain and four water channels.

The sun is blazing and we look forward to the coolness of the moon.
Continuous bathing exhausts the water reservoirs; the sunset is lovely
and brings thoughts of languorous love. This is the hot season,
Oh my beloved!

KALIDASA

Detail of page from a dispersed *barahmasa* series from Bundi, late 17th century. Gouache on paper. The sun shines on the roofs of the mansion and on the garden, with its Persian water wheel.

The month of Shravana (July/August)

During this month of Shravana the streams filled by the monsoon rains look lovely while rushing along to unite with the sea. The creepers clinging lovingly to the trees enchant the eye. The restless lightning flashes all around while flirting with the clouds. The peacocks, with their shrill cries, announce the union of earth and sky. All lovers meet in this month of Shravana. Why then, my love, even think of going out?

KESHAVA DASA

Page from a dispersed *barahmasa* series from Bundi, late 17th century. Gouache on paper. A lover and his beloved sit conversing in a room while outside the sky is black with monsoon clouds, among which slither bright strands of lightning. The rain pours on a lush garden, to the delight of the peacocks, the cranes and the frisking cows pacing near a pool. A group of women, one carrying an image of the goddess Parvati on her head, celebrate the Tij ('Third') festival. It is said that on the third day of Shravana the goddess Parvati completed her penance and was reunited with her husband Shiva, and that anyone worshipping her on this day will be granted anything they wish.

The mighty rain cloud is his charging elephant, the lightning is his banner, the rumbling thunder his kettledrum. Like a king, the rainy season, dear to lovers, has come, Oh my beloved!

The peacock folk, always charming and desirous of love, unfurl their vast and splendid fanned tails to dance more elegantly than ever in the troubling ardour of courtship.

Kalidasa

Detail of page from a dispersed *barahmasa* series from Bundi, late 17th century. Gouache on paper. One of the most felicitous themes of Bundi painting is the magnificently lush, sensuous gardens, filled with innumerable flowering creepers, shrubs in bloom, elegant bamboo thickets and majestic plantains, and teeming with all kind of birds. Here, under a sky dense with rolling black clouds and punctuated with decorative lightning, a peacock perched in a tree exhibits his open tail, a proud symbol of love.

The month of Asoja/Ashvin (September/October)

During this month the spirits of the ancestors descend to earth to be propitiated. It is the time to worship the nine Durgas for prosperity in this life and future salvation. The kings and their pandits set out to visit their territory. After the monsoon the sky is clear and in the pools the lotuses are in full bloom. The moon brightens the night, and Lord Vishnu and his consort Lakshmi engage in their celestial dance. In this month of Asoja, which is like the playground of love, why leave me alone?

KESHAVA DASA

Page from a dispersed *barahmasa* series from Bundi, late 17th century. Gouache on paper. The couple seated in a pavilion and fanned by an attendant are so absorbed in each other that they are oblivious to all that is happening outside. The upper part of the page is filled with a moonlit scene in which Krishna dances his circular dance, multiplying himself so that there are as many Krishnas as there are *gopis*. Meanwhile a victorious king and his troops return to their capital city, its citadel soaring above rugged cliffs, under which a group of Brahmins worship the goddess Durga. The mood is dramatically different in the lower right foreground where at sunrise, in the seclusion of a grove near a river, a nobleman and his companions perform ceremonies in honour of the ancestors.

The month of Karttik (October/November)

Woods, gardens, rivers, earth and sky are bright, illuminated by the Divali lamps; merriment reigns supreme over days and nights. Lovers spend their time in festive gambling. Rich and poor vie with one another to decorate their houses for the arrival of the goddess Lakshmi. A clear light pervades the whole creation: men and women are under the spell of love. This is the month to cleanse oneself in a holy river, to give alms, and to worship God. My love, do not leave home in the month of Karttik.

Keshava Dasa

Page from a dispersed *barahmasa* series from Bundi, late 17th century. Gouache on paper. A mood of celebration suffuses this painting: the night sky is blazing with the fires of thousands of oil lamps. Lovers admire the distant cityscape from the terrace of their mansion and play chess in a brightly lit room to the accompaniment of music. In a distant pavilion a couple play *pachisi*, while women bathe in the river near a shrine. A peasant, clad in a blanket, squats near the fire in the quiet of the garden.

The whole universe is plunged into
darkness, if my lover is far from home.
Oh wretch, will you come back now?
And now, everybody celebrates the festival
of lights!

Detail of page from a dispersed *barahmasa* series
from Bundi, late 17th century. Gouache on paper.
From a beautifully lit terrace a couple admire a
distant cityscape on Divali day. The city walls,
mansions, temples and other buildings, both
within and outside the perimeter walls, are
illuminated by thousands of earthenware oil lamps.

The month of Pausha (December/January)

During the month of Pausha no one likes icy water, cold food, light dresses or an unheated house. Frost pervades earth and sky. This is the time when rich and poor alike enjoy a massage with oil, cotton padded clothes, *pan*, fire in the room, and the company of young women. Days are short, nights are long: it is not the time to quarrel with one's lover. My love, do not leave home in the month of Pausha.

KESHAVA DASA

Page from a dispersed *barahmasa* series from Bundi, late 17th century. Gouache on paper. The sun is very low on the horizon on a cold winter day. A lover dressed in winter clothes sits conversing with his beloved on a terrace, with a brazier for warmth. A heavy blind of quilted white cotton at the door below keeps out the draught. In the courtyard two men, one wearing a shawl and the other clad in a blanket, squat as they warm themselves at an open fire, while in a nearby house a man is massaged with oil.

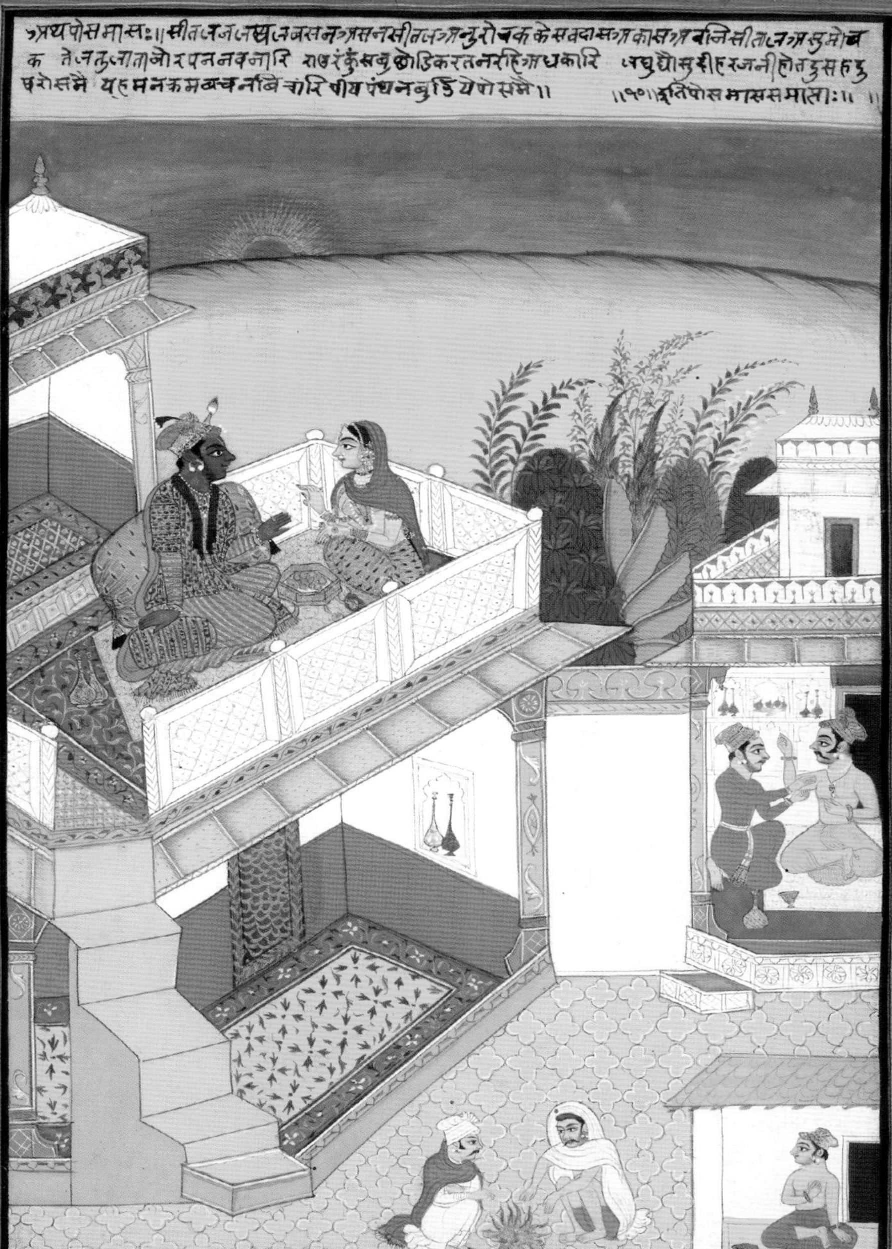
अथ पोस मास:॥
॥१०॥ इति पोस मास समाप्ता:॥

Thick blankets and rich food dressed in butter are prepared in every household. But my clothes do not protect me from the cold, unlike those my husband would have brought me from his travels. I thought he would have returned on seeing the frost. This is the season when everyone, rich and poor, remains at home in the arms of his wife.

Detail of page from a dispersed *barahmasa* series from Bundi, late 17th century. Gouache on paper. As the sun sets on a cold winter day, a man dressed in padded winter clothes sits with his beloved on a terrace, with a brazier for warmth.

The month of Phalguna (February/March)

Rich and poor make merry together without a care for social conventions. They speak freely, without restraint or sense of shame. In every home young men and women play *holi* with great abandon and gusto: they knot their garments together in a mock wedding ceremony and rub *gulala* (rose-scented red powder) on each other's faces. The perfume of scented powders fills the air. Why leave home now, in Phalguna, the month of merrymaking, my love?

KESHAVA DASA

Page from a dispersed *barahmasa* series from Bundi, late 17th century. Gouache on paper. One of the most riotous celebrations of the Hindu calendar is the *holi* festival, marking the onset of spring. A couple sit in the moonlight on an upper terrace playing with their child, who is held by a nursemaid. Below a group of men are singing near a huge bonfire, accompanied by a tambourine and hand-clapping. In a garden another couple and their entourage play *holi*: the lover embraces his beloved while she pours a flask of coloured water over his garment. Their companions, singing and beating the tambourine, squirt colours on them.

In the extremely cold month of Phalgun only the roaming wind retains its strength. I would bless Destiny if Lorik would come back to me: I am dying of cold, but his embrace would restore me to life. In every house the young women prepare the *dandahar*. Bless them, these happy princesses. Their lips are red with betel juice, and their eyes blackened with kohl. Their hair partings, their heads, their breasts and their clothes are covered with *sindhur* (vermilion, a sign of wedded status). They dance the *phagu*, and their resounding anklets proclaim their wedded bliss. My bodice and my dress, however, are reddened by tears of blood: Oh Sirjan, go and tell Lorik that his Maina, like Holika (a demoness whose effigy is burnt in the *holi* bonfire) is reduced to a heap of ash!

Detail of page from a dispersed *barahmasa* series from Bundi, late 17th century. Gouache on paper. A couple and their attendants celebrate *holi* with music, dance and squirting coloured water.

A lady awaits her lover at a tryst in the forest (*utka nayika*). Despite his promises, he has not arrived at the trysting place, so she addresses her sylvan surroundings:

Oh brother bower, Oh friend jasmine, Oh beloved mango tree, Oh night, compassionate mother, Oh darkness as loving as a father — tell me why my lover, whose countenance is as bewitching as the rain cloud (Krishna), has not come.

I drenched myself in the rain, dwelt in the depths of the forest, worshipped Kama (god of love) with sandal paste and flowers, passed a sleepless night, forgetting my modesty. What penance have I not done? And still, my Lord does not bless my eyes with his presence.

BHANU DATTA

Garhwal, Panjab Hills, *c.* 1775. Gouache on paper. A crescent moon dimly lights the forest glade where a young woman sits uneasily on a bed of leaves. With one hand she draws her dark blue veil to her face. Around her the features of the natural world — birds perched in the tree branches, cranes fishing in the pool in the foreground, a grazing deer and the colourful riot of blooms — contrast stridently with her troubled state of mind.

How can someone separate you from me: your soul from mine?
Distance makes no difference,
The kite may float and fly where it will,
But, at all times, it is attached to someone's hand.

Kangra, Panjab Hills, *c.* 1820. Gouache on paper. Kite-flying is part of the sun festival of Makara Sankranti, celebrated in mid January. Its aim is to bless the husband with longevity and children – especially sons. Men would sometimes send messages attached to kites that, ingeniously manoeuvred, would fall at the feet of the girl. This painting shows Krishna flying a kite on a terrace in the distance, while Radha stoops to grasp its shadow. Its sudden appearance reminds her of Krishna's presence and is perhaps a symbol of their awakening love.

Oh pearl of the nose-ring, thrice blessed are you; there is no limit to your good fortune!

No enquiries have been made into your lineage, your rank, and yet day and night you taste the nectar of her lips.

Colour, fragrance and softness all merge in her: a rose-petal on her cheeks loses its identity.

Her hue is golden, and the saffron paste mingles indistinguishably with her complexion: only its fragrance proves its existence.

BIHARI LAL

Kalighat (Kolkata), *c.* 1860. Portrait of a lady unveiling. Watercolour on paper. Half-length portraits became popular in India through the influence of European painting but also indirectly, through Mughal portraiture — itself prompted by European prototypes. This is the portrait of an idealized but particular woman, perhaps the heroine of a play, whose effigy was mass-produced and sold as postcards along with those of other personalities of her time.

The text on the back of this painting reads:

While looking at her image in the mirror, she is agitated. She concentrates in the innermost of her heart (in expectation of the coming of her beloved).

The complete couplet reads:

She has fixed the trysting place with her lover. She is blue-complexioned and beautiful in every limb, having applied the sixteen elements of make-up. She sits eagerly awaiting his arrival, looking at the door. Clad in red garments, she concentrates her mind on him.

LACHHIMAN

Leaf from a dispersed *ragamala* from Malwa, central India, *c.* 1630. Gouache on paper. This painting of a lady adorning herself (Vilaval *ragini*) may express her anxious heart anticipating the union with her lover. It may, however, also suggest that she is so lost in adoration of him she has ceased to see her own features in the mirror and instead can only conjure up his face. Mirrors play an important role in Indian love poetry: often the first glance of the beloved is caught in a mirror, and in a number of paintings lovers are shown looking together at their reflection, as if to stress their union.

The text on the painting reads:

With the flowery bow of Sunada (Kama, the god of love), sated by the nectar of the lips of the beloved asleep on the couch, this is the radiant Vibhasa whose plan is successfully accomplished.

Page from the 'Manley *Ragamala*' album, Amber (?), *c.* 1610. Gouache on paper. The name Vibhasa, mentioned in the text on the painting, means radiant, full of light, and may refer either to the dawn, the appropriate time in which this melody is to be performed, or to the mood of the lovers. A youth armed with a bow made of flowers and a lotus-tipped arrow tickles a sleeping young woman to awaken her and resume their amorous activities. The couple here are identified with the love-god Kama and his wife Rati.

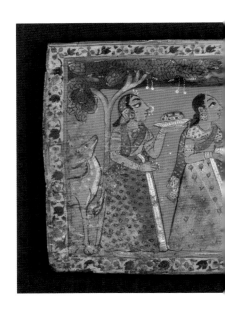

After struggling through the night,
She seemed wasted by the arrows of love.
She denounced her lover bitterly
As he bowed before her, pleading forgiveness.

JAYADEVA

Painted book cover from Bengal, from a manuscript dated 1647. Pigments on wood. Radha sits in a despondent attitude in a pavilion. Leaning on a large bolster she supports her head with her left arm, looking away from Krishna, who stands near the pavilion in a repentant attitude, with folded hands. Two of her companions try to mollify her while two others accompany Krishna, carrying trays in their hands. In the background are trees, birds and deer.

Gaur *ragini*

Tormented with love, preparing a couch of delicate blossoms, she anxiously awaits the arrival of her beloved. She casts agitated glances hither and thither. Of dusky attire or complexion, such is Gaur *ragini* of Megha Malhar.

Gaur *ragini*, page from a dispersed *ragamala* from Malwa, central India, *c.* 1640. Gouache on paper. A young woman, tormented by the pangs of love, walks alone, as if in a trance, through a forested path. A *vina* rests on her shoulder and in her hand is a flowering bough. Over her courtly dress she has donned a peacock-feather skirt and hat, as if to suggest that she has renounced the world for the solitude of the forest, where peacocks and deer are her only companions. The allusion to her dusky attire or complexion indicates that she is a *virahini*, a lovelorn woman.

Biting my mouth in love play,
since to talk would be to let go
my lord would speak only
with his hands.

KSHETRAYYA

Her face is like the moon.
(Just so)
To drink her lips is like sipping
Essence of Eternity
(Indeed)
But grabbing her hair in a frenzy to kiss her with fire and delight:
What's that like?

BHOJA

Couple embracing, from Tamil Nadu, south India, 17th century. Ivory.

A lady braves the storm and darkness to meet her lover (*abhisarika nayika*). The heroine speaks to her confidante:

Oh friend! For a young woman eager to meet her sweetheart, even the clouds are like sun, the night as day, darkness as light, the forest as her own home, and pathless wilderness a smooth way.

BHANU DATTA

Garhwal, Panjab Hills, *c.* 1780. Gouache on paper. A young woman dressed in a red skirt and draped in a blue veil walks through the forest during a stormy night. Her head is turned towards a snake slithering from a branch, and her carefully reddened toes are almost crushing the head of another. The lightning in the sky, identified in Sanskrit poetry as the wife of the cloud, suggests the imminent union of the lovers.

The text on the painting reads:

Sitting on the summit of the sandalwood mountain, the lovely one is robed in peacock's feathers, wearing a splendid necklace of pearls and ivory, and drawing towards her the snake from the sandalwood tree. She wears it proudly, as a bracelet – her body ablaze with dark splendour.

ASAVARI *ragini*

Page from the 'Manley *Ragamala*' album, Amber, *c*. 1610. Gouache on paper. The Asavari *ragini* conveys the mood of unfulfilled love and longing. Its unusual visualization – a woman dressed in peacock feathers, charming snakes – may hint at the possibility that the origins of this musical mode might originate from the Sabara people, who traditionally lived in the jungle and whose occupation was to catch and charm snakes.

Girl playing with a peacock

He left me saying he would return tomorrow,
I covered the floor of my home
Writing repeatedly 'Tomorrow'.
When dawn returned, they all enquired:
Tell us, friend,
When will your tomorrow come?
Tomorrow, tomorrow, I lost all hopes,
My beloved never returned.
Says Vidyapati: Listen, beautiful one,
Other women lured him away.

VIDYAPATI

Kangra, Panjab Hills, c. 1830. Gouache on paper. A lady has long been waiting for her lover, who has not appeared. The string of pearls she wore has become as hot as burning embers, in the pangs of separation and unfulfilled desire. She offers it to a peacock, symbol of the absent lover. The sparse background reflects her loneliness.

The resourceful mistress
(*vagvidaghda nayika*)

These are the words of the *nayika* to a traveller:
In this heat, it would be best for you, Oh traveller, to rest on the banks of the river, there, where the rows of jasmine entwine the *tamala* trees.

BHANU DATTA

Page from a dispersed *Rasamanjari* series, Basohli, Panjab Hills, *c.* 1695. Gouache on paper. The words of the heroine may sound strange to Western ears, but her reference to the jasmine creeper entwining the *tamala* trees is a clear invitation to the traveller, here identified as Krishna, to make love to her. The poetic image of the tree entwined by creeper is a metaphor for sexual union. The heat of the day is suggested by the large fan in Krishna's hand.

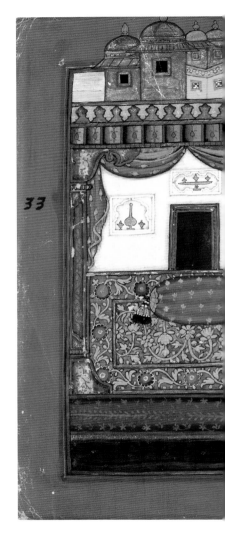

Listening to my moans as you touch certain spots,
The pet parrot mimics me, and O how we laugh in bed!

You say, 'Come close, my girl'
And make love to me like a wild man, Muvva Gopala,
And as I get ready to move on top,

It's morning already!

KSHETRAYYA

Lovers, 16th century. Ivory plaque from Orissa.

Girl playing with a yo-yo

She keeps moving to and fro, even for a short moment she never stops.
She keeps flitting back and forth like a yo-yo.

BIHARI LAL

Guler, Panjab Hills, *c.* 1760. Gouache on paper. This painting illustrates the
restlessness of the thoughts of a young girl – no longer a child and not yet a
woman – symbolized by the steady moving up and down of the yo-yo.

Dipaka *raga*

The text inscribed at the back reads:

The fourth melody, Dipak. New youth and new beloved – a tender girl filled with fresh passion. By abandoning his body and mind to her, Dipaka forgot himself and was conquered.

Lachhiman

Leaf from a dispersed *ragamala* from Malwa, central India, *c.* 1630. Gouache on paper. In the central room of his sumptuous mansion Dipak, whose name means 'lamp' or 'flame', sits on the bed fondly embracing his new love. Standing in rooms to the left and right are his four wives, who carry various objects the couple may need. Dipak's new passion, young and bashful, extinguishes the burning oil lamp on a shelf on the wall.

In search of Krishna: Singing aloud Krishna's praises, they sought him, wandering like demented women from forest to forest, enquiring from the trees: 'Have you seen Madhava (Krishna), giving you delight by the touch of his hands … ? Reveal to us, whose minds are distracted by separation from him, Krishna's path … ' Thus the bewildered *gopis* raved, with their hearts fixed on him, and began to re-enact the sports of their Lord.

Bhagavata Purana

Illustration to the *Bhagavata Purana*, from Malwa, central India, *c.* 1690. Gouache on paper. The lovelorn *gopis* are shown either wandering aimlessly through the forest or re-enacting Krishna's exploits, such as the lifting of Mt Govardhana and the killing of the demoness Putana – both in the middle register. At the centre of each register is a large flower or shrub surrounded by a string of bees, a classic metaphor for the union of lovers.

Immersed in the sorrow of renunciation, she has adopted the garb of an ascetic: sitting in yogic posture, clad in a deerskin, her body covered in ashes, and her hair matted. She has renounced all worldly enjoyments and counts on the day her lover is due to return.

Vangala *ragini*, page from a dispersed *ragamala* from Bundi/Kotah, *c.* 1750. Gouache on paper. This emaciated ascetic, performing penance in a pavilion in the middle of the lake, conveys the state of mind of a woman separated from her lover. The lover's absence forces the beloved to a new intensity of concentration. *Viraha*, separation, deepens love, and in a similar way the remoteness of God inspires feelings of deep religious emotion. The background of the painting conveys the opposite mood – love in union – thereby enhancing the ascetic's *tapas* or penance: the pelting rain revives a lush garden filled with animal life. The stormy sky, criss-crossed by lightning, suggests the courtship of lightning and cloud, and the peacock perched on the roof of the building is symbolic of love, as is the heron couple on the shore.

On this auspicious day,
Full moon in the month of Markali,
Come beloved young maidens
Of blessed Ayarpati, come adorned with jewels,
Come all who wish
To bathe in the limpid waters.

Dark-bodied one,
Fiery face like the sun,
Soft as the moon,
With eyes like pink lotus;
That young lion,
Child of Yashoda of beauteous eyes,
Son of Nandagopa
Ready with the sharp spear,
That Narayana himself
Will fulfil our desires.

Come join us in this Markali vow,
All will applaud you.

Fulfil, Oh song, our vow.

ANTAL

Detail from page from a dispersed *barahmasa* series from Bundi, late 17th century.
Gouache on paper. The poem refers to a vow undertaken by young unmarried girls
who bathed at dawn in the cold waters of a river or pool throughout the month of
Markali (mid December to mid January) in order to be blessed with a happy
married life and children. Here the girls pray to obtain Krishna (the dark-bodied
youth with lotus-shaped eyes and the figure of a young lion) as their husband.

Mother, give me my Girdhari,
My mountain-bearer!
I do not long for jewellery,
or for costly clothes,
nor do I long for a palace or
for a mansion.
I swear by the lotus feet of
Girdhar,
Dearer to me than my own life:
It is Girdhar, my Lord, that I
yearn for,
ever and ever again.

MIRA BAI

Krishna lifting up Mt Govardhana,
from Bikaner, c. 1600. Gouache on
paper. The focus of Mira Bai's
passionately intense devotion was
Krishna, in his aspect of lifter of the
mountain, Giridhara. The god is
shown effortlessly lifting up Mt
Govardhana in order to shelter his
followers from a storm unleashed by
the god Indra, here seen riding on his
elephant in the top right corner of
the painting.

In praise of Vishnu

My master with shining hair
who wears a garland, sandal, and a sacred thread,
who holds a conch and a wheel,
showed me his love
and took my life-breath into his heaven —
his great eyes are red lotuses,
his mouth, red as ripe fruit,
is a red lotus,
and his feet are red lotuses, too —
his body is burnished gold.

NAMMALVAR

Vishnu, from Andhra Pradesh (?), late 18th century. Pigments on cloth. Among the many aspects of Vishnu sung by Nammalvar is this one, Venkateshvara, whose famous temple is on the Tirumala hill near Tirupati in Andhra Pradesh. As described in the poem, the god carries in his upper pair of hands the discus and the conch, while his lower left hand is placed on his thigh, and the lower right is in the grant-giving position. Floral wreaths hang from the shoulders of the richly bejewelled image, shown in a shrine decorated with lotus garlands.

I am a mass of sin:
Thou art purity;
Yet thou must take me as I am
And bear my load for me.
Me death has all consumed:
In thee all power abides.
All else forsaking, at thy feet
Thy servant Tuka hides.

TUKARAM

Page from an album on European paper watermarked 1820, from Tanjore or Tiruchirappalli, *c.* 1830. This is a drawing of Vitthala, a form of Vishnu especially worshipped at Pandharpur (Maharashtra), to whom the poem is addressed. The focal point of the town and of Maharastrian devotional movements is the Vitthala temple. Four times a year, but especially between the end of June and the beginning of July, large pilgrimages attract a vast number of Marathi-speaking pilgrims from all parts of India. Typical of Vitthala are the straight stance and the lower arms resting on the hips.

విశ్వరూప మహావిష్ణు

Bhairavi *ragini*

The text on the reverse of the painting reads:
Ragini Bhairavi, wife of Bhairon. On the shore of the Manasarovara lake, Bhairavi in ecstatic mood expresses her deep devotion to Siva, the god of gods, whose head is adorned by serpents.

LACCHIMAN

Page from a dispersed *ragamala* from Malwa, central India, *c.* 1630. Gouache on paper. A lady and her companions are engaged in the worship of the Shiva *linga* – seen here decorated with floral garlands enshrined in an elaborately depicted temple, sited on the shore of a lake filled with lotuses. The lady in front of the *linga* rings a bell, while her companions beat a barrel-shaped drum and cymbals, working themselves into an ecstatic frenzy. The flowering trees, bending at different angles, echo the movement of the three ladies.

When I was born and learned to speak
I was overcome with love
And I reached your red feet
Lord of gods, lord with the splendid black throat
Will sorrow never end?

KARAIKKAL AMMAIYAR

Metal stamp depicting the footprints of Vishnu, from Bengal (?), 19th century. The poem refers pointedly to the reddened soles of Shiva's feet. Feet and footprints of gods, goddesses and saints have been objects of veneration for a very long time. The feet of hallowed beings are the nearest and most accessible part of their body for humans, hence the notion of 'reaching a deity's feet', meaning salvation. This stamp, probably used by devotees to stamp the auspicious footprints of the god on their own bodies, shows the four main attributes of Vishnu at the corners (clockwise from bottom left): mace, conch, discus and lotus flower. On the soles are the various objects connected with the god's career.

In praise of Shiva

I wear a cassia garland
and cling to Shiva's round shoulders,
locked in his embrace. I swoon
and then we quarrel like lovers.
His red lips make me giddy with longing,
my heart melting. I search everywhere
and fix my thoughts on his feet.
I wither
then I blossom once more.

Let's sing about the red feet of the lord
who dances
flame in hand . . .

MANIKKAVACHAKAR

Shiva Nataraja, from Tamil Nadu, early 19th century. Pigments on cloth.
The poem refers specifically to Shiva in his form as Nataraja, king of dancers.
The upper right hand of the god carries a drum, symbolic of the sound which
created the universe; in the upper left is the fire which will cause its destruction.
The lower left hand points to the deformed creature, ignorance personified,
crushed beneath his foot, and the right pointing upwards indicates eternal
salvation. To the right of Nataraja is his spouse, the goddess Shivakami. The
building in which the divine couple are enshrined is flanked by priests and devotees.
The most important temple dedicated to Shiva as Nataraja is in the south Indian
town of Chidambaram, where Manikkavachakar is said to have lived for a time and
where, according to his biography, he disappeared into the holy image.

BIOGRAPHICAL NOTES

ANTAL (9th century) is one of the great figures of Tamil poetry. According to tradition, she was found and adopted as a daughter by the great Vaishnava poet-saint Periyalvar. At first she was not included among the Alvars, the poet-saints of Vaishnava inspiration, but she later found a place among them. She refused to marry a mortal, having chosen as her husband Lord Ranganatha, the aspect of Vishnu worshipped at Srirangam. Eventually accepted as the god's spouse, she vanished in front of the holy image. She composed two works, the *Tiruppavai* and the *Nachchiyartirumoli*. Parts of the latter, in which the poet dreams of being Krishna's bride, are still sung at Vaishnava weddings in Tamil Nadu.

Bhagavata Purana (9th–10th century) is one of the most important *puranas*, collections of 'ancient stories' and repositories of mythological, astrological, religious and ethical traditions. The most relevant sections are those dealing with the life of Krishna, also known as *Bhagavata*, 'the Blessed One'. It stresses the importance of *bhakti*, self-surrender to a deity (in this case Krishna), and interprets the *gopis'* love for him as an allegory of spiritual devotion.

BHANU DATTA (late 15th century) was born in Tirhut (Bihar), the son of the poet Ganeshvara, and lived in the city of Mithila. His major achievement was the composition of 138 Sanskrit couplets, the *Rasamanjari* (freely translated as 'Posy of Delights'), in which he explores various types of lovers and romantic situations. His ideal lovers are Radha and Krishna, and a century later his work was the basis for the *Rasikapriya* by Keshav Das of Orchha.

BHOJA OF DHAR (1010–*c.* 1055), one of the great kings of the Paramara family, ruled in the region of Malwa (now Madhya Pradesh). Under him the Paramaras attained imperial status, but in addition to his political and military acumen he was also a versatile scholar and great patron of learning and the arts. Among his works are treatises on poetics, rhetoric, philosophy and politics.

BIHARI LAL (1595–1663) was born at Govindpur, near Gwalior, and spent his youth at Orchha. Eventually his family moved to Mathura where, during a visit of the Mughal emperor Shah Jahan, he had a chance to display his talent. He was invited to the Mughal court in Agra where he met Jai Singh I who, impressed by his poetic skills, invited him to his court at Amber (Jaipur). There he composed the *Satsai*

('Seven Hundred' couplets), short compositions in Hindi, which are about the love between Radha and Krishna – and their physical beauty, estrangements and reconciliation – as well as the comments of their friends and servants who carry messages between them.

JAYADEVA (12th century) is known as the last great name of Sanskrit poetry. Traditional accounts of his life claim he was born to a Brahmin family, possibly in Bengal. He became an accomplished Sanskrit scholar but abandoned that life while still a young man to be a wandering mendicant devoted solely to God. However, his ascetic life ended when a Brahmin of Puri insisted on giving him his daughter Padmavati as a wife. It appears the pious Brahmin was acting on the instructions of Lord Jagannatha: Padmavati was a dancer in the great temple dedicated to Jagannatha at Puri, and Jayadeva shared her devotion to the god. His *Gitagovinda* skilfully weaves song and recitation together into a pastoral drama which vividly portrays the intensity of the love between Radha and Krishna, in all its nuances of longing, passion and separation.

JAYASI (16th century) is the name given to the Sufi poet Malik Muhammad Jaisi, whose fame rests mainly on the *Padumavati*, a work he composed in Awadhi *c.* 1520. It is the oldest extant narrative of the famous story of the heroic Padmini of Chitor, one of the most popular Rajput romantic tales. Its long story ends with the princess and all her royal ladies throwing themselves into the fire to escape dishonour and captivity, while the men die in a last desperate attempt to defend Chitor. The *Padumavati* is one of the seminal texts of Awadhi literature and was so popular that within a century it had been translated into Bengali.

KALIDASA (5th century) means 'the servant of Kali'. No facts are known, but many legends have been woven around his name. Supposedly handsome but dull, he was not well educated. He was to marry a princess, but she was appalled at his coarseness. In desperation he called for help from his tutelary deity, the goddess Kali, and was rewarded with wit and sense. His is undoubtedly the greatest name of Sanskrit drama, and the *Raghuvamsa* ('Raghu's genealogy') is generally acclaimed as his best work. Another charming work is the *Ritusamhara*, the 'Cycle of seasons', which describes the six seasons of the year and their changing aspects.

KARAIKKAL AMMAIYAR (mid 6th century), meaning 'the lady or mother from Karaikkal', was one of the great figures of early Tamil literature and one of the few female saints included among the poet-saint followers of Shiva, the *nayanmars*. Born in the small town of Karaikkal on the shore of the Bay of Bengal, she was a great devotee of Shiva from childhood. She married, but her sanctity awed her husband, who left her, remarried and had a daughter. Pleased that he had resettled, she asked Shiva if she could become a skeletal figure, like the goblins who danced around him on cremation grounds. She later lived in Alangadu and remained there until her death. She signed her forceful poems, which are often filled with gruesome imagery, as Karaikkal *pey* (the goblin from Karaikkal).

KESHAV DAS (Keshava Dasa) (1555–1617) was a native of the Bundelkhand region in today's Madhya Pradesh and became a poet at the court of Birsingh Deo, the Bundela king of Orchha, in whose honour he composed a eulogy. His most famous work is the *Rasikapriya*, a composition on erotic art and different types of 'heroes' and 'heroines', the *nayakas* and *nayikas*. The 'hero' is almost always Krishna and Radha the 'heroine', and he describes them with great relish and sensitivity of feeling. His other major work is the *Kavipriya*, a treatise on poetics, which contains a section on *barahmasa*, the description of the twelve months of the year.

KSHETRAYYA (17th century) was a Telugu poet who seems to have wandered through-out southern India. His name has been explained as deriving from *kshetra*, meaning temple or holy site. His signature, however, refers to Muvvagopala, which may relate either to Gopala (i.e. Krishna) in the village of Muvva or 'Gopala of the jingling bells'. His poems are about courtesans and their lovers and were probably intended for performance. Their customer is the god Muvvagopala, and the intimacy of feeling between god and devotees is expressed in a sexually explicit language.

LACHHIMAN (late 16th to early 17th century?) is named in a number of *ragamala* paintings, the oldest of which date from the mid 16th century and were painted in Malwa (now in Madhya Pradesh). However, nothing more is known of him.

MANIKKAVACHAKAR (9th century) means 'he whose utterances are rubies'. He is one of the four most important personalities among the Tamil Shaiva poet-saints. An unusually gifted youth, he followed in the footsteps of his Brahmin father, becoming a minister of the Pandya king of Madurai. In the course of his political career he met a guru (Shiva in disguise) and, instructed by the guru, he ignored his duties and embezzled the king's funds to build a Shiva temple. The incensed Pandya initially imprisoned him, but a series of miraculous events persuaded him to set Manikkavachakar free. The saint spent the rest of his life wandering from temple to temple singing the praises of Shiva. He composed many of his impassioned hymns at

Chidambaram during his last days. He is said to have disappeared in the sanctuary of Nataraja, merging into his chosen deity, the dancing Shiva. One of his major works is the *Tiruvachakam* (Sacred Utterances), a collection of hymns in praise of Shiva.

MIRA BAI (1498–1546?) is the subject of a number of legends which claim she was a princess from the Rajput state of Merta and was given in marriage to the Rana of Chittor, one of the most powerful Rajput states. She had surrendered herself to Krishna at a very young age and refused to fulfil her wifely duties, incurring the wrath of her husband and his family. The situation worsened when she became a disciple of a low-caste saint, Raidas. Attempts were made upon her life, but she was always saved by divine intervention. She composed and sang songs in praise of Giridhari (Krishna in his form as supporter of Mt Govardhana), reputedly passing her days and nights in front of her beloved god's image. Eventually she moved to Vrindavan where she spent the rest of her life worshipping Krishna. According to tradition, the image she worshipped eventually came to life and ordered her to follow, at which a fissure opened in the earth and both the image and the poet disappeared into it.

MULLA DAUD (14th century) was a Muslim poet who composed what are now among the oldest documents in Awadhi, also known as 'Eastern Hindi': the fragments of a romantic poem called *Chandayana*, dated AH 779/AD 1377–8. Born in Dalmau, near Kanpur in Uttar Pradesh, Mulla Daud was a disciple of the Sufi saint Jainuddin. The *Chandayana*, composed under the patronage of Jauna Shah, a minister of the sultan of Delhi, Firuz Shah Tughlaq, was based on a popular folk ballad of northern and eastern India. It narrates a dramatic story of love, betrayal, magic and separation for the hero Lor (or Lorik) and the heroine Chanda. Mulla Daud was probably the first of several poets who, inspired by romantic tales and ballads, reworked them into allegorical poems according to the tenets of the Sufi tradition, which by the fourteenth century was firmly established. Unfortunately, the *Chandayana* lost its poetic and mystical appeal in the seventeenth century and was only rediscovered in the 1920s.

NAMMALVAR (9th century) can be translated as 'our *alvar*'. Probably the greatest among the Tamil poet-saints, followers of Vishnu, he was born in a small town in southern Tamil Nadu, now called Alvar Tirunagari in his honour. According to tradition, his parents abandoned him in a temple before an image of Vishnu. He then walked to a nearby tamarind tree and sat beneath it, remaining utterly silent, for thirty-five years. Eventually Madhura-kavi *alvar* found him and posed a difficult question. Only then, it is said, did Nammalvar break his silence, accept

Madhura-kavi as his disciple, and commence singing his rapturous hymns in praise of Vishnu. One of his most celebrated works is the *Tiruvaimoli*.

SUR DAS (Surdasa) (1478?–1563?) is one of the most renowned Hindi poets. He composed his poems in Braja *bhasha*, the much-loved form of Western Hindi spoken in the districts around Mathura. Blind from birth, he was reputedly the son of a Brahmin singer and a disciple of the philosopher Vallabha. Even in his lifetime he was highly regarded as among the most prominent singer-poets of India, with a following at the Mughal court. Among his few surviving works are the *Sur-sagar*, a series of lyrics inspired by the Krishna theme, and the *Suravali*, a collection of devotional lyrics.

TUKARAM (1607–49) was born at Dehu, a village near Pune, the son of a grocer. He became a devotee of Vithoba of Pandharpur and neglected his domestic duties – unsuccessful in both domestic and business life, he became a wandering mendicant. Throughout his life he was persecuted by the Brahmins for the unconventional religious ideas expressed in his poetry. Most of his hymns, *abhangas*, couched in Marathi, are in praise of Vithoba. His inspired devotion made him famous and attracted masses of devotees. He was a favourite of the great Maratha ruler Shivaji, although he never accepted invitations to visit the court. It is said that when he felt the end of his life was approaching, he drowned himself in a river. Even today, pilgrims going to Pandharpur sing Tukaram's compositions.

VIDYAPATI (1352?–1448?) was born into a Brahmin family in Mithila (now in northern Bihar), where his father was attached to the court. Nothing is known of Vidyapati's younger years, but he probably followed the usual pattern of young Brahmins, learning Sanskrit and verse-making. His first commission came from Kirti Simha, king of Mithila, in 1370, and through his friendship with the heir apparent, Shiva Simha, he was able to compose more than five hundred love songs in Maithili. Writing poetry not in Sanskrit but in the language of the common people was a major departure from accepted standards. These highly inspired poems were composed between *c*. 1380 and 1406. Both highly erotic and devotional, they swept through eastern India, enchanting audiences with their psychological insight and warmth of feeling.

FURTHER READING AND SOURCES

Translations adapted or reprinted from published sources as noted below.

Assier de Pompignan, R. H., *Meghaduta, Rtusamhara*, Paris 1967, pp. 52, 57, 59, 74 (*Ritusamhara* ch. I, st. 1; ch. II, st. 1, 6; ch. VI, st. 1)

Bahadur, K. P., *Rasikapriya of Keshavadasa*, Delhi 1972

Bhattacharya, D. (trans.) and W. G. Archer (ed.), *Love Songs of Vidyapati*, London 1963, p. 49

Cutler, N., *Songs of Experience: The Poetics of Tamil Devotion*, Bloomington and Indianapolis 1987, pp. 119, 143, 168–9

Dahmen-Dallapiccola, A. L., *Ragamala-Miniaturen von 1475 bis 1700*, Wiesbaden 1975, pp. 79, 245, 322, 340, 393

Dallapiccola, A. L. and E. Isacco (eds), *Krishna: The Divine Lover*, Lausanne 1982, p. 193

Dehejia, V., *Antal and Her Path of Love: Poems of a Woman Saint from South India*, Albany, NY 1990, p. 43

Dwivedi, V. P., *Barahmasa: The Song of Seasons in Literature and Art*, Delhi 1980, pp. 129, 130, 131, 133, 135, 136, 138, 140 (*Kavipriya* ch. 10, vv. 24–5, 28, 30, 31, 33, 34)

Ebeling, K., *Ragamala Painting*, Basel, Paris, New York, New Delhi 1973, pp. 140, 144–5

Ingalls, D. H., *Sanskrit Poetry from Vidyakara's 'Treasury'*, Cambridge, MA, reprinted 1972

Jha, Amar Nath, *The Veiled Moon*, New Delhi 1973, pp. 45, 47, 54–5

Macnicol, N., *Psalms of Maratha Saints*, London, New York, Calcutta 1919, p. 65

Narayana Rao, V. and D. Shulman, *A Poem at the Right Moment: Remembered verses from premodern South India*, Berkeley, Los Angeles, London 1998, p. 90

Ramanujan, A. K., V. Narayana Rao, D. Shulman, *When God is a Customer: Telugu Courtesan Songs by Ksetrayya and Others*, Berkeley, Los Angeles, London 1994, pp. 121, 127

Randhawa, M. S. and S. D. Bhambri, *Basohli Paintings of the Rasamanjari*, New Delhi 1981, pp. 31, 73–4, 93 (*Rasamanjari* st. 23, 61–2, 78)

Stoler Miller, B. (ed. and trans.), *Jayadeva's Gitagovinda: Love Song of the Dark Lord*, Delhi 1978, p. 106 (pt 8)

Tagare, Ganesh Vasudeo (ed.), *The Bhagavata Purana*, vol. IV, Delhi 1978, pp. 1443–4 (bk X, pt IV, ch. 30, vv. 4–13)

Vaudeville, C., *Barahmasa: les chansons des douze mois dans les littératures indo-aryénnes*, Pondichéry 1965, pp. 44, 46 (*Maina Barahmasa*, st. 407, 409), 58 (*Nagamati Barahmasa*, st. 348)

ILLUSTRATION REFERENCES

Photographs © The Trustees of the British Museum, Department of Asia (OA)